Thank you for healing what hurt the most.

Inspiration

I was at a place in my life, a place that seemed so familiar.
I felt as though I had the world in front of me,
but from time to time I felt like something was going to go wrong
and I was merely holding on.
Do you know what it feels like to be needed? I do.
I think it is one of the most graceful feelings a human can feel.
But I also think that when that feeling is taken away,
you somehow forget how to feel.
I don't know if I'm making sense,
I guess I'm writing whatever is at the forefront of my mind,
and my heart.
When I was little I used to think the world was a beautiful place.
It is.
As I've grown up, I have witnessed that beauty with my own eyes
and that is what I now live for.
Sunsets. Sunrises. Rain. Roses. Storms.
And everything after it.

A collection of my words are written in this book.
Read them. Relate to them. And write your own if you wish.
Writing has given me a silent voice.
A way to express myself without speaking.
Thank you for being part of my journey.
Love, Silentperception.

i was there.
but i was not.
i don't think many people
would ever understand that.

You and your heart deserve
so much better than what
you have been through.

May peace come
for your pure heart.

Go take a walk in the rain.
Trust me, it heals.

-some advice from SP

The beauty of not giving up,
the beauty of trying again and again.

-resilience.

A lesson I have brutally learnt, endurance.
To learn how to endure is probably one
of the most difficult lessons I have learnt.

And I am still learning.

You told me that you knew me
and I laughed inside
because I knew it was not
possible for you to know me,
when I do not know myself.

Most of us have the choice
to choose what we deserve.
Don't ever forget that.

If you were not meant to be his
then you never really were.

i am still waiting for
your heart to leave mine.

Give me the stars,
and I will give you
my heart.

You deserve the world,
even if I am not meant
to be a part of yours.

Maybe his stars were
never meant for my sky.

I hope you don't forget us.

I wonder if I will ever find
the good in our Goodbye.

I need you on the days
that I do not need myself.

I was so lucky to have
been loved by your heart.

-thank you

i was afraid that i would not be me
without you.

walk away so it will be easier for me
to let you go.

I prayed for someone to love you in all the ways I couldn't.

wanting someone who doesn't want you is like holding onto someone whilst they're begging to let go.

I have learned that
people will still leave
even if they love you.

You will always be in my
heart even if I have left yours.

Let me be
your safe place
again.

we had left each other's lives.
but we had stayed in each other's hearts.
and I think that was the saddest
thing of all.

He was looking at the stars,
and I was looking at him.

Just because you love someone
with all of your heart,
doesn't mean they will love
you back with all of theirs.

come home to yourself
before you go looking
for it in someone else.

He will find somebody. He will.
I believe that with all my heart.
He will find someone that loves him,
more than I ever could.
I'll know and so will he,
because she won't walk away like I did.

I may have stopped praying for us,
but I will never stop praying for you.

There was nothing I wanted more than to love you.
But there was nothing you wanted more than to leave me.

the hardest part for me was learning how to not
be a friend to someone that didn't want me anymore.

I have knocked enough times to realise
that it is not me you wish to let in.

Do you know how many times I have wanted to run?
I have just been so afraid that you will not follow.

I will always love what cannot escape my heart
even if it will not love me back.

There is a wall between the two of us
that you are not willing to break.
And there is me standing on the other side,
quietly calling your name.

Every few days I lose you all over again.
And I have to learn to be okay with that.

Trying to fix something that
was meant to stay broken was
one of the hardest things
I have ever had to learn.

I wonder if the world knew how happy you made me.
I wonder if it was the world that took you away from me.
Maybe it was my fault, I showed the world that you meant the world to me.
Maybe the world took you because it knew what you meant to me.

do you know how many times
i have picked up the phone to call?
and then stopped at the very
thought of you,
not loving me anymore.

You asked me if I missed you.
I missed you every single day.
But I missed you most in my darkness,
because you were the only one who stayed.

There is a sadness in me
that was only ever meant to
be understood by you.

she loved what was never meant for her.
and i think learning that was the hardest part.

I pray that God takes away
the pain I left you with.

Sometimes I feel like talking to you, just to pick up where we left ourselves. But I know that you won't talk to me in the same way anymore, and then I realise that maybe silence is the only thing we were meant to have left to share.

You and I both know,
our hearts have too much
between them to ever
let each other go.

some bonds will never break
no matter how far you drift away.

And if I saw you again I would tell you that I am so sorry for hurting you.
I should've spent my time undressing your wounds.
I should've let myself in and poured love into your soul.
I should've helped you heal.

I should've helped you heal.

My heart has loved your heart since
you came.
And it will continue loving your heart,
even if we never speak again.

Maybe,
in another world
my heart will mean

to find yours.

Sometimes, love means that you have to let go.
You have to let go.

The hardest part was not letting you go.
It was being so familiar with the pain that came after.

-the aftermath

I believed that I was not made for this life.
Then I found you and I realised,
you were not made for it either.
And from that moment,
I could not stop my heart from loving yours.

i don't know what hurts the most.

missing you.

or knowing, that you do not

miss me back.

I still hope that you will come home to me.

I wish I could love without
wanting so desperately to be
loved in return.

How strange was it?
How we wanted the same things.
But we were never meant to
have them together.

My life is so quiet without you.
I almost wish you would come
knocking on the door so that I could
let you in and love you all over again.

For you to be happy without me,
is what I wished for in the end.
But damn, it hurt.

There are very few people
who understand your soul
without your voice being heard.

Where do the broken souls go?
I want them to find me,
and take me home.

You cannot begin to understand
what goes on in my mind.
But that isn't the sad part.
The saddest part is that I cannot
make you understand,
however much I try.

Darling, do not hold on if he leaves you. I know that you will be sad, and it's okay for a little while. If you are to be sad, then be sad that he has lost you. Be sad that someone as precious as you will not be replaced no matter how much he may try. And I know that you will feel like it is the end of your world, but you will learn that the people who were never worthy of your love were never meant to stay.

We are often misunderstood. When strangers begin to become our friends, we learn things about people. Beautiful things like their sadness. We learn how it is not just us who feel lonely sometimes. It is not just us who crave to be loved. To be accepted.

Acceptance.

We learn the importance of acceptance. We all have flaws. We are imperfect. But what makes a friendship, what makes love, is accepting who we are when we're not smiling, when we're not happy. And it is those people, the ones who look past our flaws, the ones who better us and help make us everything we are meant to be, it is those who we should keep. I have always believed that even in brokenness there is beauty so if ever you come across someone who shares the same soul as you, look for that beauty before you deem them broken.

He loved the Sun and I loved the rain.
He used to say that he could see the Sun in my eyes.
I had waited years for somebody to see beyond my sadness,
and when they finally came, I wanted rain.
When I used to hear it, I would run to my window to watch it fall.
I would close my eyes and dream of someone who would sit beside me,
someone who would understand what the rain meant to me.
The Sun came, but I could not help but stay in the shade.
I had waited years for the Sun, and then it came.
And all I wanted was the rain.

-rain

She had always loved the stars, for they gave hope to her darkness. She loved the way the sun set everyday because each day was different. Some days she felt overwhelmed by her sadness. Some days she felt like her day was a sweet one. She loved with every part of her. But her love was not always the best to her. She made mistakes. She would overthink, and at times she thought that would be the death of her. She just wanted to be loved. She wanted to be accepted. She never wanted to be understood, she just wanted someone to learn who she was. She knew she had God and she believed that He would heal her heart. She had just come from a storm, she had fallen in the rain, she had given all she could. But she loved what she unwittingly destroyed. And she was sorry for that.

You and I is something I won't forget. We were something special.
I believe our two hearts met for a reason.
Time was never meant to be on our side, but love was. Love is.
God gave you to me.
And even though it was for a short while, it felt like the world.
Like we had known each other for years
and you were on your way home, back to me.
You may not be here now.
Your mind and your heart may have taken you away from me
but I will never be far from you.
Once my heart loves, it cannot let go.
And my heart loves yours.
It will always love you.

Tell me that it gets easier.
The absence of you. The sadness in me.
Tell me the Moon will give me the light I seek for.
That the stars will shine straight into my soul.
It has been so long since you left you and I.
Tell me it will be okay.
That one day I'll wake up without the thought of your name.
Tell me one day you will understand why
I left the kindest love I have ever known.

The kind that I will spend my life searching for.

some hearts don't leave; they stay until they realise that the pain is only going
to get stronger. that the effort is only going to get harder.
and that the grief of mourning someone
that is still alive is only going to hurt more every single day.
some hearts don't want to leave.
but sometimes the heart that you so desperately
want to be in, has already taken you out of theirs.
that heart has let yours go.
and now you must learn how to do the same.

"How do you stop loving the one who left?"

You don't. You can't. You learn to live with it because it becomes a part of you. After a while it's normal for you to feel a certain way. It's normal for you to miss the one thing you want, the one thing you can't have. As time goes on you realise that no matter what you do or however much you try, the person you love will stay in your mind. You learn to be without the one you love because you go on with your life and you hope that someday soon you'll feel happy again.

i wanted so much to fall back into your life. like nothing had changed.
like the distance between us didn't leave us emptier than we had ever been
before. i wanted so badly for your heart to need mine again. for the stars to
shine from your eyes like they used to when they met mine.
for the Moon to be the one thing we talked about.
i wanted you to be everything you had ever been.
the whole of you. not half.
i wanted to hear your laugh,
my favourite sound.
but it had never been about what i wanted.
i learnt that the hard way.
and after all the time we had apart,
i thought that maybe your heart would be safer
with me not around.

I wish that I could've told you that it would've been okay.

The distance never took you away from me, because you were still there.

You were still there, right before my eyes but I couldn't seem to get to you.

I don't know if that was because you didn't want to or if I wasn't reaching out enough. I think I always knew that I would never be able to let go of us.

Let go of you.

I wish that I could have loved you the way that I was supposed to, the way that I was meant to.

They told me to follow my heart but what if my heart led only to you?

What would I have done if the one person who understood me was the one I broke?

My heart was so full of you, my heart is so full of you.

I was never scared of losing you,

I was scared that you'd stay with me even after you'd gone.

And you've gone.

it had taken time for me to come back to myself. when he left, i left with him. and that meant that i had left myself. everything inside of me didn't feel like home anymore. i had made him my home. it was as if i had a cage around my heart, i had chosen to lock it myself and hide the key because i never wanted to feel that way again. and i knew by locking that door, nobody would ever come close enough. some call it bravery, they talk about the courage that falls from your heart. i was never either of those things.
i was just a girl who was so afraid of calling somebody else mine,
even if i was never meant to be his.

nobody told me how once you love with all that you have, you never quite get it back. they told me how time heals your wounds. the ones you cannot see, the ones that bleed. they told me how the pain is supposed to teach you and will only make you stronger. they told me that even on my darkest days i would find light. or better yet, light would find me.
but nobody told me this. that in the early hours of the mornings, i would find myself searching for you in every part of me that i had lost. nobody told me that you would become a memory i wish i forgot. they didn't tell me how it would feel on the days i needed you most but you would not be there. nobody told me how a single word from you didn't feel like you were coming back.

it felt like you never left.

I wanted to thank him, something I had never done before. Had it not been for him, I would never have understood what it truly meant to fight a war within myself. I wanted to thank him for disappearing for days at a time. It was then that I learnt how to be sane and alone. I wanted to thank him for listening to my words but never quite knowing what to do with them. I wanted to thank him for making me feel like the only woman in his world. And then for making me feel like the loneliest woman in my own. I wanted to thank him for holding onto my hand and then quietly letting go. I wanted to thank him for the darkness, for the light I longed for. Had he not taught me all of these things, I would never have understood how it was okay to love something, that in the end, I was always meant to let go.

It must have been years since I last saw you, it must have. It must have been years since we last spoke. It didn't feel like that today. Today I saw you. I saw that you saw me before I had seen you. I felt the uneasiness, the fear.

I wonder if you would have ran if you had the chance. I wonder if you wished that you did not look back.

Over the years, I had so much left of you in my life, in my days, and in my heart.

And then I saw you, I saw my best friend, the one that made me smile, the one I felt safe with and everything we had ever been through to get to this point, this moment, felt like it didn't matter.

It didn't matter anymore.

We spoke like strangers; nobody would have known that our souls had found each other in what seemed like another lifetime.

You smiled and I smiled back, but it wasn't your smile that made me sad. It was the look in your eyes, the kind of look that told me that I was still there.

We hadn't spoken for years, but it felt like the first. It felt like the first time in that moment, where it was just you and I.

-i knew i'd see you again.

I was a child of love. An old heart at such a young age was what I believe was a blessing in disguise. I thought I loved someone that loved me back.
I thought he was
the one.
Time taught me that he wasn't. Trust taught me that if I were to break, I'd never be whole again. And he taught me that loving someone was my biggest mistake. I would constantly get asked why I didn't just let him go, why I didn't walk away from the one thing that caused me pain.
My reply was simple, I couldn't let go.
What was worse was that I didn't want to.
I could not face leaving what made me whole, but what also broke me.
But then the apologies would come and I would accept every one.
We told ourselves it would never happen again, but he knew. I knew.
See, I had built this wall to protect me, but it seemed like the more I tried to save myself from the hurt, the more it backfired on me.
I don't know who I feel sorry for more, the man that is meant to truly love me or my inability to let someone in. I came to the decision that in the end, if I were to settle with someone that does not deserve me, then maybe, maybe,

I will be free.

I waited for you because I knew God heard me
when I told Him I wanted to love someone with
the whole of my heart and not just with the pieces
I had kept from another man.

The world seemed quieter without you.
It was still sweet, the sunset filled my heart with everlasting peace.
And the rain still made my soul smile. But your absence left me feeling like I was missing something. Like a part of me had disappeared one night and never thought to return. I thought that I was important. I thought I meant something more than to become a stranger to you again. It was okay. I was kidding. But it had to be okay. I had to wake up every day knowing that today we may not speak, tomorrow may be the same. I had to smile like I had the world at my feet because I could not find a soul that would understand who you were to me. And so I went on, I held you in my heart because I knew that was the only place you'd never leave. I would be happy, and I prayed with my heart that you would be too.
Without me.
My days were so full of laughter and light,
it was so easy to hide that part of my life.
But my world was quieter without you.

My world was not my world, without you.

You are often on my mind. In fact, you never really left. You have stayed in my heart since the day we met. There are days when I try not to think of you at all. But you come, you let me miss who we were. I see you when I sleep sometimes, I see you when I smile. I wish you could hear about my day again. Remember when you used to listen to all the crazy things I'd say? It's selfish of me because I have everything I need, but still my heart aches for your love. Maybe if you called and listened to my voice at the end of your phone, I'd know.

I still read the letters you wrote to me, I find it hard to believe those words were once true. Do you believe in love they ask me, I will always believe in it because of you. I know I have to let you go. Maybe I will. Maybe just a small part of me won't. I wonder if you know that there are a thousand reasons why I want to call you, but there's one reason why I don't.

There was a time when he was in my life that he left for a while.
6 months it was.
No warning, no goodbye, just silence.
I wondered what I had done and how he was okay without talking to me.
Was his heart not breaking like mine?
I used to laugh when they told me I was 'the best' for him but they didn't see from his side that I was never enough.
I learnt two things from his absence, two things that I'd like to share with you.
Firstly, it was never about needing me, it was about wanting me.
Need is when you feel you cannot live without someone, want is so much more.
Secondly, he had left without any words.
Nothing to tell me that he'd be back, nothing to tell me that I should wait.
I learnt that if he could do that to me, if he could leave me, his dearest friend, then anyone could.

Holding on to what was never meant to be,
for a long time has been a part of me.
I have prayed for you what I pray for myself,
love, peace and happiness.
I hope that life is kind to you.
Remember those dreams you told me about?
I hope every single one comes true.
No matter where we are, or where you go,
think of me, read my words.
I have loved you with the whole of me.
Letting go, setting you free, is the only thing I have left to do.
Look to the Moon on the nights you can't sleep,
you know that I will be looking at it too.
Maybe we'll find our answers,
maybe we'll find ourselves.
Let it take you to where you're meant to be,
let it take you home.
May light shine in the darkest corners of your heart,
for the rest of time you will be in mine.

Can we sit under the stars and talk about you? I want to know who you are. I want to find out things about you that you've never told anyone else. I want to learn what makes you smile, I want to know what you crave for. Is it knowing what touches a soul because that's what I like too. What is it that you hide in your heart? What is it that you keep silent about? Tell me what your eyes see, tell me what your mind says. Let's sit under the stars for the night, I want to know what it feels like to love you.

I wish my heart could understand what my mind has already learnt. You were not for me. No matter how much I wanted you to be, no matter how much you told me you were, we were not meant to be.

I wish my memory of you would disappear into the night or out in the cold, somewhere instead of the place you called home.

I am a mess. Some would say a beautiful mess wrapped in love that has no idea where to go. My intention was never to hurt you but I am the one that left. I wish I could take our story and write it all over again. Instead I write what you'll never see. I think I got caught up in the idea of us I forgot about what it takes for two people to become one.

Trust, hardship and sacrifice.

We fought alone and never together. Occasionally you come back and I sit with the thoughts of you and I. I can't help but wonder what we were, and who I have become after giving you my heart.

All I ever wanted was the life I saw when I looked into your eyes, but I needed God. If I knew then what I know now, I wouldn't think twice,

I'd pick the second one.

When we first met I remember wanting to know certain things about him. Not the normal things people talk to each other about but those rare things that never get asked. Like if he had ever loved or how he got that scar near his eye. I wanted to know his favourite colour and what made his beautiful laugh. I wondered if he found peace when he saw the Moon or the sunrise. I wanted to know what would be on his mind if he ever woke up in the middle of the night. For years we were strangers in the same place, I saw who he was with everyone, but I craved to know who he was when he was by himself. I wanted to love his soul, and for all the parts he didn't love, I wanted to love them for him. He used to tell me things he was too afraid to tell himself and as I began to heal his wounds, mine slowly disappeared.

All along he thought that I'd saved him, if only he knew that is was him, who saved me from myself.

It seems like yesterday, the day we first met. Everyone remembers that day. The day you meet the person that changes your life. I remember our first conversation. You asked me what my favourite colour was, then you smiled when I said black because you thought I'd say pink. The more I learnt about you, the more I realised that you saw everyone in the same way, but me, I knew you saw me differently. I adored you. I still think of you. I still smile to myself when the moments we shared cross my mind. I still laugh because of you. You always made me laugh. I miss that. Laughing with you. I hope you're happy. I'm sorry I can't be there to watch you grow into the man I knew you'd always become. I hope that if you ever think of me, you smile. It still hurts, I know, but that's because we both loved. I know it's too late for us, I still believe you're destined for greatness. We will be okay without each other. I always remember you because you don't forget the one who changed your life. You don't forget that person.

It wasn't the world that
made her tired.
But many
of the things inside it.
What was in her heart,
was always heard,
by every soul lucky enough
to be in the shadow of her
presence.
Her brown eyes told me
a story.
They spoke about battles,
about the kind of wars she
had been in.
You could never tell,
unless you were smart
enough to read between
her lines.
Cold, heartless, bitter.
The facade they put on.
But she never had to do
that,
she was known by
the kindness of her heart.
Her soft voice was made
to soothe the ones that
were broken.
And her words, well
whoever read them
would know it.
It is her, the Moon
we look up to.
It is her, the one we
run to.
It was her.
The definition of beauty,
from a thousand
broken pieces.

You are always here even though you have left. Sometimes, I hear your voice telling me it will be okay especially on my bad days. Sometimes, you sit quietly, waiting for me to remember you. There are times when all I want is to hear you call my name. All I want is to be needed by you. I often find myself thinking about what you were to me, what you still mean to me.

Life takes from us what we love, it takes from us what we must learn to let go. I guess I am still learning. All I hope for you is peace. Peace, the very thing we never stopped yearning for. And I hope you find it. Find it for us.

You are gone, but you are still here. I feel you with me, I still feel your soul standing next to mine. And I know this because I believe that God wouldn't have put you in my heart, just to one day, take you out.

And I just wanted to tell you that you changed my world. You came and you took my thoughts into your hands and helped me understand why certain things happen. You told me sweet words and you listened to me cry.
I'm telling you this just in case nobody has ever told you because you deserve to know that you changed my life for the better.

Try not to wish that what happened to you never happened. Try not to despise every hardship that comes your way. Because whatever you're going through or whatever you have gone through was all meant to happen. It was all meant to make you who you are.

It will be messy, it will hurt and it will sometimes make you question everything you believe in but always remember one thing. If you believe in Allah, if you believe He is above us, taking care of each and every one of us, then nothing can stop you from being happy. Nothing can make you feel any worse, because He will make you better. A time will come when you will be thankful for everything you wished had never come your way.

You will be happy and you will learn to smile again.

"Listen to me."

He had the kind of voice that made everything seem like it was going to be okay. After everything I told him, I expected him to have a sympathetic look on his face. I thought he might have told me that I deserved better. Instead he smiled and softly said,

"Listen to me."

"You remind me of the Moon.

See, the Moon was made for souls who have lived in darkness. You have given hope to them, just like the light of the Moon has. You are so far away from people; they are close but you're nowhere near. Your words and your thoughts tend to have one person in them."

Everything he said after that made sense, as if he knew what I was too afraid to say. I watched in awe, the way his eyes stayed in mine, he took my hand and placed it into his.

"You carry this notion around, like you don't deserve to be loved again. Again? Darling, that was not love. You will know what it feels like to be loved and when you do, this sadness will no longer be your home. You remind me of the Moon. You are beautiful and wise and you are who they look to when they are lost."

He smiled as I turned away to wipe the tear from my eye.

"Everyone needs someone who reminds them of the Moon, you were not his somebody, nor were you meant to be his Moon."

I waited for him, he was the only man I wanted to love. He knew the language to my soul. He'd often talk about life and how strangers understood the secrets we kept in our minds.

I fought for the words he kept close to his heart because I wanted to know the man he was. There's something about a man that's been wounded before. His scars told stories that I never thought a woman like me would know the meaning of. I admired his courage,

I admired his honesty. And when he laughed, everything inside of me laughed with him.

I feared his love, I feared the intensity. But I waited because I knew how it felt to be loved by a man like him, a man that caught fire from those around him, but never let a flame touch me.

I was waiting for him to find me. I wanted him to see the sunset in my eyes. The place he could go when he felt nothing but emptiness. If he knew me, if he really knew me he would've known I was the one he could have run to. For years he came in and out of my life. Seasons changed, the nights became long and after every conversation we had I hoped this time he would finally understand. I did not love him because I had to, I loved him because I wanted to. My heart and his became friends. The sound of his laugh stayed with me long after he had gone. Maybe we were meant to be this way after spending together what felt like the best years of my life. In these moments he comes and goes, a place I sit and reminisce. He only filled half of the pages, I wanted him to find me but instead I found myself. I thought my story would end with him by my side but now I know that space is meant to be for someone else.

they tell us to move on, to be patient with our hearts and to let them heal slowly.
they tell us it will be okay, and that everything happens for a reason.
they search for something inside of us that left along time ago.
they think we will be happy and often I believe so.
but they aren't with us when we are with ourselves.
they don't feel what we feel deep within our souls.
they can't possibly understand how it feels to stop loving something we thought was meant for us.
we smile. we laugh. we allow them to paint a perfect picture of us, we let them believe in love.
because maybe it's meant for them.
it just wasn't meant for us.

I didn't know what it felt like to love someone who was no longer there. Nobody ever told me how I'd feel if I saw him again. They didn't tell me how I wouldn't sleep the same and how everything that happened to me after him wouldn't hurt as much as it was meant to. I had known loss, the type you cannot forget. No matter what I did or who I wanted to be, he was something that never left me. It stays with you. You're not the same person, you'll convince yourself that you are, but you won't be. You'll see life differently. You'll open your heart to strangers, you'll laugh with your best friends but you'll be reluctant to let your heart love again. He was never mine, if I could ask him anything then it would be this; for him to love me for a little while longer, maybe then I could have been his.

The thing about him wasn't his inability to love me. I learnt how sometimes the love you give isn't always the kind you receive. It wasn't his heart because I knew how big it was. There were storms but sunshine always came after them and that's what made me happy. I chose to stay by his side because I thought he was meant for me. After he'd gone I still felt the tiniest part of me holding onto the hope that maybe he was. I loved him but there were days I felt so lonely, I remember I began preferring my own company. I had settled with what I thought love was because I had never known any before his.

I wait. But I do not know what I'm waiting for. As I sit in the stillness of the night, I look for something, anything to ease this ache that has found a home in the pit of my stomach. I wonder, what am I trying to find? And why is it taking so long? The memory of him who I loved returns at the same time, every night. The memory of the woman I once was haunts the person I am right now. She used to laugh, and after laughing she would feel better, like someone had put the life she was losing back into her. But now there is only a small hope that she will come home. Was it home if where she is now feels like she never really belonged? How does she tell those who ask her what's going on in her mind when she has no idea? It's just another fragment of her heart. I wait. And she is waiting to be found.

you were 17 and you met a boy you thought you belonged to. you saw in his eyes what you'd never seen before. you saw yourself, a beautiful reflection. when he asked if you were okay, you didn't have to say a word because he already knew what it felt like. he knew you could've said you were fine a thousand times but he wouldn't have believed it. you cannot seem to let him leave, he's always there wherever you go. you look for peace, you try to find something that will take away the pain but you know yourself that he was the one. you're afraid that nobody can love you like him, you're afraid that you won't learn to love again. but you have to remember that if he loved you like he said he did, he would've shown it, he wouldn't have ran.

"How did you know it was him that you loved?"

I always smiled when someone mentioned him. It was something I did. No matter what my mood was or how I felt, the thought of him would make me feel better. My reply wasn't going to be the usual.

"When you know someone is the one, you just know."

He was more than that.

"How did I know? I knew because he wanted to know me. Not the me that everyone knows, but the me that hardly anyone knew. When I felt like I was losing myself, he helped me find all that I had lost. Everybody needs somebody, that's what they say, but I chose not to believe it until he saved me. We laughed together a lot, I'd tell him my secrets and he'd laugh even more. Have you ever watched someone you love, laugh? One of the best feelings in the world. I'd tell him to stay up even though I'd fall asleep, in the morning I'd wake up with a blanket over me. He didn't have to say 'I love you' because he did that in a thousand ways. Like saying 'don't forget your coat' or 'let me wipe those tears from your eyes.' It was all the little things that made me admire the man he was. And that's how I knew, it was him that I loved."

I could never tell if he really loved me. When I say that I mean, was I the woman on his mind constantly? Or was that space kept for someone else? I'll never know, sometimes I wish I did and other times I think it's best this way. The love I gave to him was never quite like the love I received, but I didn't mind. I thought, if I could love him with everything I had maybe he'd actually see me one day. See my soul and how for him it was a home. It was never my choice to love him, that happens. You fall in love and for a while you're the happiest person in the world. And then I began to lose him. It took me three years to realise it. I chose to stay because I wanted to. Because I knew a man like him deserved to be loved. I had so much love to give, but him and his heart never had the strength to hold it.

Sacrifice. I think this word is the most beautiful act of love. At the time I did not see the beauty in it, but now I do. When I was younger I always knew that the man I would only be with would be the man I'd spend the rest of my life with. But how are you sure when you're young and naive? That's why I sacrificed my love for him because I stood by everything I believed in. I thought maybe, if I wait, if I let him go we can still be friends. And we were, for a while, we were. But then he found love in the arms of another, he found something that I could not give him. I thought maybe he'd come back when his nights were lonely, maybe I'd be the one his heart would lead too. And he did just that, when she was not there. I stayed for a while as a friend, but we both knew we were something more. Me and you, we always were. I sacrificed what I felt for him because I knew it was the right thing to do. I knew I could not have the best of both worlds, and I knew I would be the one who always got hurt. I thought at the time I'd have everything to lose but as I've grown into the woman I am today, I've learnt that by sacrificing my love for him, I had everything to gain.

I used to wish he knew what he meant to me. I used to wish that just for a second, he could see himself from my eyes and know how special he was to me. I thought maybe if he knew, he'd understand the love I had for him was pure. The kind of love I had for him, I'd never felt for anyone before. The first boy that came into my life, we were kids back then and I was just a young girl. It was a blessing to have known a man that I thought I'd spend my life with. Till this day it's still a blessing but in a different way. He taught me all I needed to know about love and how it works. I just wish he knew what he meant to me, maybe I could have done more. One of the greatest lessons I've learnt in life is how to live without the one you once loved and although it may take you down the darkest paths, it will lead you back to where you belong. Some days I feel like the wind is calling our names, other days I feel like we were only meant to be left with that memory in a frame.

After him there was nobody else. People, they tend to move on and find a home in another heart. But for me it was different. I grew to find comfort in my own company. I felt safe in my solitude. Love was given to me and even if it was for a short while, I understood it. They used to say that you don't leave the one you love no matter what. But you do, sometimes you're with the wrong person and sometimes love just isn't enough. When I saw what it had done on those nights I couldn't sleep, I imagined the epilogue in my book, 'love wasn't meant for me.' This didn't mean I hadn't dreamed of taking care of another soul. It didn't mean I craved to be alone. Sometimes I wanted to be held, sometimes I wanted to be somebody else in another person's eyes. Love had taken all that I had. I was afraid that if I gave what I had left of my heart to another man, then maybe this time, I wouldn't get it back.

I wanted him to be happy. I always knew that. On the first day we met I looked at him and I could not stop smiling. It's like we had known each other from another lifetime.

You know me, I was fond of the stars. After we had become friends, every time I looked up into the sky, I thought of him. I saw his face, his brown eyes and his laugh. I loved his laugh.

If I could have made him the happiest man, then I would have. I cannot walk away from you without telling you how much I tried. It made me sad for the longest time. But I knew in my heart that he'd find love again, in another woman's eyes, in her heart he'd find what I could not give him.

Silence became a part of who we were and then we parted ways. I never forget to pray for him, I never forget to pray for his happiness even if in the end, he could not be mine.

I never used to know what to say when they spoke about you. It's like your name fell from their mouths so easily. It was a natural thing to do because whenever there was me, there was you. They'd ask me how you were and sometimes I'd wish I knew, other times I'd hope you were well, happy and making the best out of the life God has given you. Some, I know were glad that you were not by my side anymore. At first that mattered to me but then I realised that they didn't know our story. They didn't know about the laughs we shared until our bellies hurt, they didn't know about the nights we cried, bearing each other's souls. They didn't know about the man you'd become since the day I first met you. And even though you're not part of my life anymore, I smile when they say your name because it may have only been for a while but once upon a time, your heart had chosen mine.

i pray for this ache in my heart to fade.
for every broken piece to find its way.
i pray to sleep again without the echoes
of my past reminding me of where it
all went wrong.
i pray for hope and peace.
i pray for the feeling after you heal.
most of all,
i pray to find who i am meant to be,
from the wreckage i have become.

I pray for the day a woman learns
how to love herself without needing
a man to do it for her.

There are days when I miss you
more than I ever have.
Today was one of those days.

-24.01.17

We wore sadness
like it belonged to us.

-you and i

I pray you get what
you're wishing for.
And if you don't,
I pray you get better.

...and I will tell them that he didn't mean to hurt me. even if everything inside of me felt like he did, he didn't. he was my best friend and your best friend will never mean to hurt you, even if they do.

I stayed. I always chose to stay. I wanted to, with all my heart I wanted what we had. When they tell you that you never know what you have until it's gone, they're right. That very thing fades away day by day and it's you that has to sit there and watch it go. That is what hurts, when they're on their way out and there is nothing you can do to stop them from going.

I tried, I always tried. But whatever I did or whatever I said somehow became words that didn't feel like they were supposed to be felt. Instead they felt like words that meant everything to me and nothing to you.

I chose to stay and maybe that was my mistake. We both knew as time went on we'd lose each other. I was holding on to us, but you were not part of us anymore. I knew that, I did but I was too scared to let you go.

I stayed. I stayed because the hope inside my heart hurt less than the thought of losing you.

I pick myself up every day. When they ask me how I survived this long, how I have no animosity for you in my heart. I tell them that I left, and by leaving I mean because I had to, not because I wanted to. I tell them that my heart has been broken but it is the smallest things that fix it. Like the rain or a new book or the look on my mother's face when my father tells her he loves her. I believe in all that I used to believe in. I know love of how it should be.
We break, we do. We heal and we mend.
They ask me how I have lived. And I keep telling myself that if I was strong enough to walk away, then I can get myself through any day.

My dearest family and friends.

She deserves the stars.
Her heart has been bruised in so many ways.
Her eyes have already witnessed so much pain.
Still, she searches for light on her darkest days.
Oh Allah, the next time You place such joy into my heart,
take some back and place it into hers.

I wish I could put you back together again but I know I cannot do as much as He can. So I tell Him about you, I tell him how you're broken and how you crave to be at peace. I tell Him how kind your heart is and how beautiful you are to me. I know He listens. I know He sees. You deserve to smile again, my dearest friend.

I used to wonder why God had blessed me with a friend like you.
A friend who was always there, a friend that I could be sad with.
A friend that never ran from the paradox that was me.
And then I realised, I realised that God placed you by my side because He knew our souls would one day search for peace. He knew that I would love you and that you would love me. He knew that no matter what, we'd overcome every hardship, we'd find the light that we both longed for and that one day we'd find peace.
God put us in the same place, He put your name in my heart every time I sat to pray. I knew from then on, no matter where He would take us, you would always be right next to me.
He put you in my heart, because that's where you always were from the start.

I pray that love finds you.
I pray it teaches you to smile.
You thought for so long that
you didn't deserve to be loved.
But you do.
Your heart may have been broken
by somebody who didn't understand
everything you are.
You have this notion in your heart that
you should be alone for the rest of your life.
But why let your love go?
When your love can change the world.
Beauty is not recognised by those
who are blind to see it.
My darling, your heart and soul
will be loved by the one who deserves it.

Sometimes I feel helpless when it comes to comforting those closest to me. I write words they may not have heard for a while, hoping one or two may fill the void that they carry.

I wish they could see how their souls have changed my life. How every time I think of a memory and laugh to myself, it is without a doubt always about them.

Friends of my heart, I hope you know you deserve to be happy. I pray whatever pain you're feeling soon disappears. You see my tears when they haven't yet reached the surface.

You take my hardships into your hands, the hands that already have so much weight to carry. I wait for the day the darkness that has found a home in you, finds light.

Even if I am nowhere to be found and even if you recognise the sadness in my eyes, know that I'll always be here. I would do anything to make you smile, anything, even if it is something like sharing your silence. To me, it will never feel like enough but I hope with all my heart, you know, my hand will always reach out for yours, forever for you to hold.

-from the heart to the homies

I wish you happiness and when I say that I mean true happiness. The kind that we do not find in materialistic things. The kind that isn't temporary and lasts only for a few moments. I wish you the kind of happiness your heart craves for. The peaceful, sweet, soft kind. The kind you can sit in silence with, the kind that mends your heart over and over again. The laughter you share with your friends, and that comfort you find in your loved ones, that kind of happiness is the kind I want for you. I want it to stay with you and when you feel sadness I want you to remember that the kind of happiness I want for you is the kind that will find you.

It is not the end, it is only the beginning for you so I pray that you have the happiest beginning.

The thought of him stays in her mind. When she talks about him her eyes shine like the ocean. Her words are full of joy and kindness. I pray for her every day. She deserves to be happy, she deserves to smile. If they are meant to be then I pray that Allah makes them one because I know what kind of woman she is and I know what a perfect wife she would be.

She was a good girl. In everything she did and everything she spoke. To him, she was an Angel. He cared so deeply for her because it was her who made him want to be a better man. She inspired him and in a beautiful sort of way he felt protected by her.

And what he loved about her the most was that she was pure. Her intentions, her mind and her heart. She wasn't like any other girl he had met before, she was a beginner when it came to love. He admired her faith and belief in Allah, through hardship and through ease she would never forget Him.

He knew that Allah had already written her story, he only hoped and prayed that he could be a part of it, that he could one day be the one to hold her hand and lead her into Jannat.

For you, I prayed for Him to take the pain out of your heart.

I am in love with the way you
think and see the world.
It is something I admire.

-from a friend of my heart

My Father once told me,
it was not me he didn't trust,
it was the world and all the people in it.

How can you be so sad
but beautiful?

-from the heart that healed mine

I feel like our souls have been
friends long before we met.

I know you, you seem to know yourself very well. I know how your insecurities have prevented you from loving yourself. I understand that you feel unworthy, I understand how the depth of your thoughts may one day destroy you.

You forget the words you so selflessly give to the ones you love. You will not be able to see that they hold a special place for you in their hearts.

I need you to understand how you are nothing you think you are. In fact, you're everything you believe you're not. Your humour, your smile and all that you use to hide yourself.

You look at yourself and only see what you have been led to believe. And I look at you and see how every single part of your soul only wishes to be loved. I look at you and hope that one day you will see, how someone like you will learn how to love themselves. And if by chance you don't, you don't believe in that day, I will be here to remind you, always my beautiful friend.

She's the kind of girl who wishes for everyone what she wishes for herself. She's the kind of girl that prays you get the best. Her heart is full of love and although it's sometimes hard for her to show she cares for others before she cares for herself. She wants to see you smile even if inside she's crying. That's the kind of girl she is. The kind you want to love, the kind you want to be friends with. She is patient, she is kind, she doesn't realise her worth sometimes. I only ever pray for her best days to come so I can be there to watch her get everything she deserves.

If I could tell you anything it would be that you do not deserve the pain you're going through, but you still go through it. And what I mean is that you wake up every day with the same knot in your stomach, with the same heavy heart as the night before and you survive. Your smile tells them you're happy, you're okay. Only those who look close enough will see that you are holding on to what hope you have left. I admire you. I see past your strength, I see past your smile. And I admire your faith. I want to tell you this and I need you to believe it. I cannot accept the fact that your ending won't be a happy one. A soul like yours is destined for greatness. Keep going because Allah knows every burden in your heart, my dear friend, He will give you ease, the kind you have been searching for all along.

My best friend. When I think about our friendship and how you've changed my life just by being in it, I can't help but smile. I can't help but have the kind of feeling inside that makes me so happy and safe. You have this beauty that your humble self is unaware of. The kindest and sweetest person I am so lucky to share my life with. You have been the kind of friend that most people wish they had. You listen to every story I tell, you laugh at every joke I make, usually at me but you laugh and that's the main thing. I love who you are and I love how you believe in me. You give me hope and you are always there with your words of comfort. I have never known a heart like yours, I often wonder how I got so lucky.

I hope with all my heart for you to be happy. You deserve to smile, you deserve to be loved. No matter what Allah has planned for you, I will be here right by your side because you are my best friend, you're the one I love with all of my heart.

-my bestest friend

The kind of friend you are:
The kind that sits in my heart.
The kind that makes the words
in my mind seem easier to say.
You stand by my side,
silently you stay.
You don't know the kind of friend you are,
the kind that doesn't need to be present
for me to understand your intentions.
You came, and I knew that Allah had
chosen for our paths to meet.
Your happiness is what I pray for,
your smile is all I want to see.
For broken souls, Allah sends Angels
and I'm so thankful He sent you to me

Him.

He sees you.
He sees your exhausted thoughts
weighing in your mind.
He sees chaos in your eyes,
so eager to reside.
He can hear your silence,
if only you knew.
He knows your hearts conflicted.
All it takes is for you to be true to yourself.
There is nothing He cannot do.
So take one step towards Him,
and He will come running to you.
-the beginning

I have spent so much of my life
searching for answers
that I should've been asking God for.

If we are meant to be
then He will bring you
back to me.

If you have God in your heart.
God will always have you.
Remember that.

sometimes i feel so weak.
there are days where i wish
that God could take me away,
maybe then i would finally be at peace.

You have to give everything you've ever felt
and everything you've ever given, to God.
You have to give it to God because
He can do what you cannot.
He can save what you cannot.
And He can give what you cannot.

Don't worry.
God knows your heart.

Just because Allah took something from you doesn't mean He won't give it back to you. If you believe that everything happens for a reason then know that Allah is the best of all planners. There is no one that truly knows what is in your heart more than Allah so be patient and trust in Him, Al-Wahhab – The Giver of All.

Sometimes I wake up and I feel really low. As a human, I have to remind myself of my faith because without my faith I would be in this permanent state. I have to tell myself that it is okay to feel the way I am feeling. It is okay if not everyone understands it, and it is a great comfort to those who do. I sit and I think about all the good things I have in my life, the things that make me smile, the smallest of things. And then I have to remember that Allah does not burden a soul with what it cannot bear. And that's when I know that it will be okay and that I am strong enough to let this feeling pass. I am meant to be where I am. And I am meant to go through these battles to make me become who I am meant to be.

Isn't it crazy that if one thing didn't happen then we'd be together? If on that day, I didn't make that choice and if you told me what I wanted to hear down the phone, then maybe today we'd be in each other's lives instead of being strangers. How different would our lives be right now? I think that's what hurts the most. The words we wished to hear and the actions that never came.
I know it happened for a reason, maybe it was a blessing in disguise.
I also know by believing in Allah, it will all make sense in the end.

I asked her once what she thought about on those long walks home and on those cold winter nights. She sat me down and smiled and told me how in the end everything was going to be alright. I asked her how she knew and what made her so sure, she told me it was Allah who had shown her the light. She told me how she loved a man that she would've done anything for, she told me that she wanted to marry this man and give him everything she could. But one day the dream she was living came to an end, because he walked away from the woman that knew him better than he knew himself. I asked her how she learned to love again and she told me with tears in her eyes that it was Allah who helped her heal. It was He who gave her hope in the darkest times she had ever lived in and it was from Him she learned there was no love greater than the love from Allah. The man she wanted to grow old with, I saw him in her eyes. I asked her how she found peace and I told her how I'd been searching for it for such a long time. She took my hand and smiled, I'll never forget these words,

'All you have to do darling, is place Allah in your heart.'

Whenever he left I felt like he had taken my heart with him.
At night I used to wait for a call, something to tell me we were going to be okay.
I dreamed about fairytales and I wished we could be one.
But I was young, I was naive and I hopelessly fell in 'love'.
I was a fool to believe it was love because love doesn't treat you like that.
I read somewhere once to never run after what doesn't love you back.
And now I understand.
I pretended we were perfect, but even something wrong seems right for a while.
I was lost. I craved for peace.
And in his absence, the woman I used to be had gone.
I lay awake thinking about all the things I should've done.
My heart was tired. My mind was a mess.
In those moments, shall I tell you what my soul ached for most?
No, it was never him.
It was God.

I had always missed him. It never mattered if it was after an hour or a few days. I was just that kind of person. We laughed a lot together. We talked about life and love and fear.

We talked about the world and the different kinds of people in it. Sometimes we sat in silence as if words did not matter. And sometimes they didn't. Sometimes it was silence that made us better. We had found one another at just the right time. God had given me an Angel, someone to help me heal my deepest wounds. And I knew, I knew one day I'd have to let him go but that would be one day and never before. They say there are reasons why people cross your path, they say only some will leave a mark on your soul. He touched mine in ways he will never know.

Some days it feels like the sadness chose to stay before it came, some days it feels like he was meant to do the same.

But I'd never wish to go back to before I knew him because at that point in my life, I realised it was him that I needed. You cannot leave the heart of somebody who only ever loved you. So I thank God for giving me that time in my life.

That time in my life, I spent with him.

I told Allah about him because I knew Allah heard every word I said. At night when the Moon arrived for its duty, I prayed he would see its light. I'd never met a man like him before, or maybe I had but our hearts were not meant. I told Allah about him because I knew that even though he wasn't in my life anymore, he was safe in my every prayer. Although I couldn't comfort him after a hard day, I prayed that Allah saw his every tear.

Sometimes Allah takes the ones we love and maybe this was our test. I know I couldn't have become the woman I am without Allah's help. I pray for him every day, I pray for him, nothing but the best. I keep my faith in Allah because I know He knows the love I long for. Maybe we weren't meant to be together, maybe just not yet.

My heart was his. I thought it was. We were never lovers, nor were we friends. We were something in between, something I was afraid to reach. It haunts me sometimes, the words I never told him. The words I never found the courage to speak. He used to come back, and I would let him. This time maybe he would recognise me, this time maybe he would see me as the woman wanting to take care of him. It happened so often but something inside my heart kept hoping that maybe this time it would be different. Even though he's gone, I sometimes wonder if a part of me will always be his. When I pray, I pray for him, he was a part of my life I won't forget. I loved a man I never had. We almost made it. But my mind, it's at peace, because now my hearts with Him. Where it always meant to be.

I want to remind you that He knows what is best. You are the quietest person in the room but He can hear your every thought. Don't think for a second your duas are unheard. He is with us every day, waiting for your call. You are not drowning in this darkness, you are simply learning how to be strong. Remind yourself of Him, my dear, that is when light is born.

But maybe your heart was made to be broken
so you could call on Him to fix it.
What better way to lose what you
thought was love, to find it all over again?

If you are a good person, don't for one second think you deserve bad. If difficulty is sent to you, think of it as a gift, think of it as a lesson. A lesson for you to learn, a lesson for you to become better. Bad things do happen to good people and you wonder what you have done, why bad has come your way when you strive to do good. You have to remember and keep in your heart that Allah tests those He loves. Bad things happen to good people, take it as a blessing and believe that good things will come.

Oh Allah, I ask You to make me a better person.
Allow me to see the good in every one and allow
me to appreciate everything You have blessed me with.
Oh Allah, I ask You to give me hope.
Allow me to see the light that is You, allow me to
see past those who have hurt me.
I ask You to help me forgive the souls that never
intended on causing me harm.
I ask You to help those who need your help and
I ask You to give ease to those who are struggling.
Protect the hearts of those I love, give them every
blessing I could ever ask for.
Oh Allah, help me.
Allow my heart to love, take away any hate that
hides within me.
Help me become the person I know I can be.

I wonder how you are, what life has given you since I left. I wonder if you lie awake sometimes like I do, thinking about our lives and how simple they once were. Thinking about the times we used to laugh every day and night. I wonder if someone else is making you smile, if someone listens to you fall asleep on the phone. I wonder, but I wouldn't want to know. Funny how it works. I pray for the happiness I know you deserve. People make mistakes especially when they're young, I learnt to forgive those whose intentions were never meant. It was only after you'd gone I questioned everything we once had, and then I remembered Allah and how He tests us all. How He watches over us and protects us from things we haven't known. I'm growing into the woman I aspire to become. Some days I wish you were by my side to grow with me. Other days I guess you were only ever there to teach me.

I used to wonder why bad things happen, especially to good people. I used to wonder why those with the warmest smiles carry burdens that only they know of. But it isn't only them that know. Allah knows. Have you ever thought that the struggles we face are His way of calling us to Him?

He knows who we are when nobody is watching. He knows what lies deep in our hearts. Only He can take our sorrows away and replace them with ease.

No matter how hard we try to help ourselves. No matter how hard we look for words of comfort, Allah will always be the one to cure our pain. I used to pray for things I thought would make me happy.

All I pray for now is for Allah to guide me. He knows best and He is who I need to trust.

I pray that Allah mends the hearts of those that are broken.

I pray for the purest love in Islam. I pray for nothing but peace.

can I tell you something about my heart?
it has been hurt before.
like the sound of waves crashing against each other, that's how it feels
sometimes.
there are not many things that calm my soul but I am thankful for the places
that feel like home.
when I cannot make sense of what I feel,
I tell Allah, I ask Him to help me heal.
when I find myself in complete darkness,
I ask Allah to let some light in.
He knows my heart, I ask Him for peace, hope and strength to get through
every hardship.
there are not many people you can talk about your thoughts with. the kind of
thoughts that are hidden in the depths of your mind. there are some that your
words fall out to, it's those who try to understand.
I love the way some hearts care about me,
I wish one day I can love like them.
the kind of love you give to another isn't the kind you give to yourself.
their selflessness, their honesty, their soul.
the kind of people that make me believe there is good left in this world.
the sound of the rain against a window and
the smell of warm coffee.
the words from poets that tell the stories of my past. laughter, the kind that
makes you forget.
my heart, yes it's broken. but what if it wasn't?
would I have fallen in love with all of these things?
I asked Him to save me, I asked Him to heal each fragment. there is nothing in
the world that I believe in more, than knowing that He will mend it.

I hope He heals your heart.

Made in the USA
Middletown, DE
04 October 2021